"Into Your Hands..."

Distillation of the Letters of Fr. Jean-Pierre de Caussade

by
James H. Kurt

© 2019 James H. Kurt. All rights reserved.

Children of Light Publications
09/14/2019

jameshkurt@gmail.com

ISBN: 978-1-7332154-1-1

No part of this book may be reproduced, stored in a retrieval system, or transmitted by any means without the written permission of the author.

Summaries of Letters that appear in:
Fr. Jean-Pierre de Caussade, S.J. Abandonment to Divine Providence. San Francisco: Ignatius Press, 2011.

Cover photo/art by James Kurt.

Author's Website:
www.writingsofjameskurt.org

Podcasting Site:
www.hermitinthecity.libsyn.com

> "Enter through the narrow gate."
>
> Lk. 13:24

Preface:
A Distillation of Wisdom

Though paraphrase is employed throughout along with de Caussade's vocabulary, there are no quotations per se and this is not so much a summary of the spiritual master's letters (over 300 pages condensed to about 70) as it is a distillation of the profound wisdom found in each. The book can be opened at any point to discover that wisdom.

The letters were all written to cloistered nuns, but no mention is made here of any of the sisters or their specific questions and problems. The short paragraph or two on each letter is oriented more generally toward souls seeking perfection; the prayer at the end of each entry is their cry.

The subject matter is gleaned from the letters themselves and accompanied in measure by the author's insights. The letters are numbered as in the book, but the titles are original.

The author had intended these reflections only for his own edification, but along the way realized they might serve the spiritual benefit of others as well. This is his sincere hope in publishing this volume.

TABLE OF CONTENTS

Preface iv
First Book 1
Second Book 6
Third Book 25
Fourth Book 34
Fifth Book 45
Sixth Book 53
Seventh Book 65

Other Books by James Kurt 73

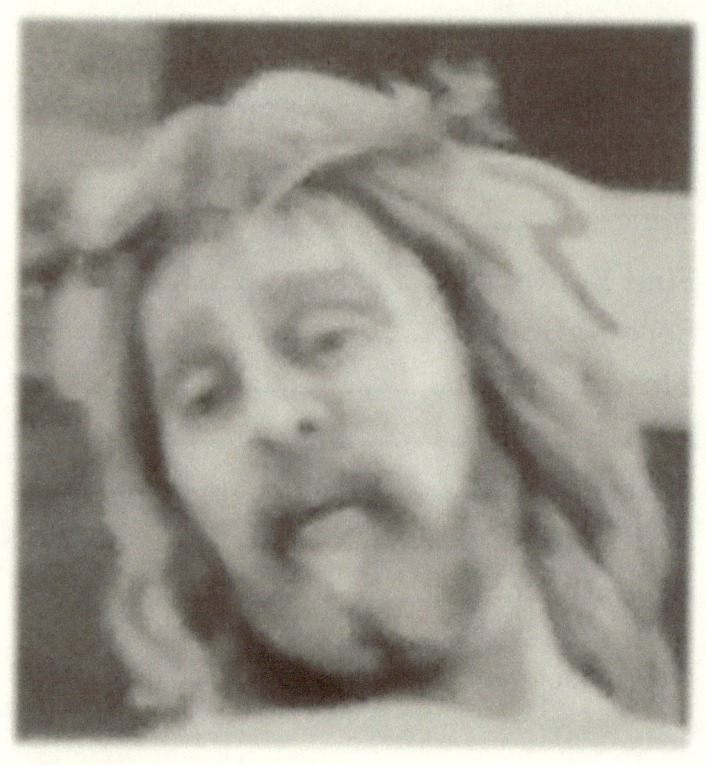

First Book

I – Abandonment

How do we abandon ourselves entirely to the will of God, accepting all that happens as coming from His loving hand, no matter the trouble it brings? The answer to this is indeed the key to peace, to absolute joy in the presence of the Lord – to union with Him.

But who is there can do this? No one, I fear; no one. Unless it is by the grace of God.

> O Lord, let your hand be heavy upon us
> if it will help us to realize your presence within
> and bring us to union with you.

II – Annihilation

O the annihilation of our own will and desires that the LORD might be all to us, that He might fill our soul with His presence! How death brings new life! O what blessing is here, though it look quite the opposite.

> To the ground let us come, O Lord;
> on the ground let us make our home.
> No yeast to raise us in our own esteem –
> in your light alone let us dwell.
> Alleluia!

III - Duty

Since we are useless servants, what concern should we have for the particular task the Lord sets before us? It matters not what we do, only that it is the will of God that is done.

And so, why should we become anxious, why should we be afraid? All must be accepted as coming from His hand as a call to accomplish His will.

Indeed, we are useless servants, and so, let us but accomplish His will.

> Lord, whatever you call us to,
> whatever you set before us this day,
> let us know it comes from you
> and do all in your Name.

IV - Home

Come the end of this life; let it take us home. It shall not be long, and so, be attached to nothing of this world.

> Dear Lord, carry us unto your Kingdom;
> let all we do lead us there.

V – Trust in God

How all things turn to the good when we trust in God instead of ourselves and our own means. Leaning on Him we are held up and strengthened in doing His will. And what more could we want? What more do we need?

But how infrequently we turn to Him; how little we are inclined to seek His help. Our whole mind must be changed to focus on Him, to look to Him, and not to go forth in our own will and on our own way.

> Lord, help us remember to turn to you,
> to call upon your Name and your presence
> to be with us and guide us in all things...
> to trust in you though we see not
> the path before us.
> Then all shall be well,
> on earth and in Heaven.

VI – Alone with God

O what joy to be with God alone, to have nothing of this world, just Him!

In this desert place we find ourselves, for He comes so close to us. There is nothing else to desire. Abandoned by the world, we have Him fully.

> Let us not be afraid to be alone, Lord;
> knowing you are there
> is all we need.
> Let your will be done in our lives.

VII – The Wonders

What can we say of the wonders of living strictly according to the Gospel, with God as our only focus and no dependence whatever on the things of this world. To live day by day and hour to hour not knowing where our next meal might come from but trusting in the Providence of the Lord and giving ourselves entirely to His will – it is the ideal. But it is quite real, and can be accomplished on this earthly plane, as the first disciples did, and as the most devout religious do today.

> O Holy Spirit, why should we have a thought
> for tomorrow?
> Are not the troubles of the day sufficient thereof?
> Do you not care for all our needs;
> do you not watch over us,
> longing for us to turn to you
> and so find you at work in our lives?
> Let it be so, I pray.
> Let it be so more and more. Alleluia!

VIII – Everything for Nothing

We give Him our nothingness, and He gives us His everything. We find ourselves in justice empty before Him, and He fills us in love with His gifts. This is how our God acts toward those who are humble before Him.

> O Lord, we thank you for your love,
> for your condescension toward our nothingness,
> for lifting us up unto you
> though on the ground we should remain.

IX – Do Not Fight God

What foolishness it is to fight the Lord or be anxious about what He ordains, for He ordains all things and we but need to accept His will.

Should we not trust in Him who loves us and holds all things in His hands? And so, what disservice we do Him to be anxious about many things. We must place all our days and all our future days in His hands, where they belong.

> The troubles of the day
> are indeed sufficient thereof,
> as you have said, O Lord.
> We should rejoice to know you watch over all
> and that we get closer to the moment
> in which you dwell
> when we entrust all our lives to you
> and desire nothing more.

X – Happy Faults

If our imperfections can serve to make us patient and humble, then for these, too, we should be thankful; indeed, the Lord can turn all for the greater good, and so we should realize this and allow Him to do so with all that befalls us.

Let us be willing to suffer as poor, simple, humble souls, and in peace we shall remain with the Lord at all times, despite the disturbances at the foot of the mountain. Too often we imagine problems that are not problems – all is according to God's will and for our best.

> Help us to be truly wise
> in our patient humility, Lord;
> help us to see as you see
> that we might see all in your light
> and so all might be for the betterment
> of our souls.

XI – Mutual Blessings

Let us wish each other only those blessings that are truly spiritual and in keeping with the will of the Lord. Let us have each other's spiritual good alone in heart. Only the Lord's peace and presence let us seek for one another, and then all will be well all our days.

> Pray, my brother, my sister,
> that all we do leads to eternal life
> with our Lord and Master.
> Let us never be separated from Him
> or one another.

Second Book

I – All Things

How can we think only of the Lord? How can we place all things, temporal or spiritual, into His hands and give them no thought? How can we die to our will and our desires, and any concern for graces?

> It is only by you, Lord, we make any progress,
> and so we give ourselves to you without reserve,
> placing even our faults into your hands.
> We know nothing – you are all in all.

II - Virtue

Let us ever fortify our virtue against any falls into mortal sin or venial sin, or even the lessening of any grace and merit in us, by being ever willing to make the sacrifices necessary to strengthen ourselves and remain in prayer with the Holy Spirit. Alleluia!

Lord, I am so little inclined to virtue,
leaning rather into sin,
but with the grace that comes from you,
virtue can become my friend
and my one desire.
Let it be so.

III – Furniture

It is the Lord who furnishes our soul with all it needs to become one of His holy ones; all we need do is remain in humble prayer before Him and allow Him to do His work.

Let your hand be upon my soul, O Lord,
to form it in your image.

IV – Practice

Let us put into practice the way of the Lord by avoiding sin and accomplishing our duty, always saying 'yes' to His will (which is ever for our good), and we shall humbly advance in the spiritual life.

We give our 'yes' to you, O Lord,
and so seek perfection in you alone.

V – The Glory of God

We must love God purely and for His own sake and glory, desiring union with Him above all and knowing it shall only come to us by His grace. Awaiting it with humble faith, let us be submissive to the Spirit, withdrawing from the senses and wishing for nothing but what the Lord ordains. Let us expect nothing but contempt from creatures, but everything good from our glorious God.

> O Lord, you are all we desire;
> let that desire ever grow
> that indeed we might find you alone.

VI – Interior Perfection

Let us seek interior perfection, remaining in peace despite our trials, accepting infirmity and illness as salutary purgation even as we practice mortification of our own inclinations. Let us profit from all God sends, zealously pursuing our own perfection but never with anxiety.

More and more interior let us become, simple as a child before its Father, loving Him with all our heart and putting up with others... in patience ready with forgiveness even as we correct ourselves.

> Lord, let us indeed become as your children,
> reflecting your glory in this world
> and in our souls.

VII – Peace

O to belong completely to God and be at peace in His presence, detached from all things and creatures and keeping firm in faith despite any darkness that surrounds us, knowing the Son shall soon return.

> O Lord, keep us in your peace,
> unafraid of any darkness.

VIII - Prayer

Prefer dryness and aridity, pause in that which humiliates you, accept distractions if you cannot collect your mind – rely on faith. Cast all fear from your soul, give but a simple glance to the heavens... the most perfect is the most simple. Run with the Lord on the way of holiness!

> How shall we be holy as Thou art holy, O Lord,
> except that we rely entirely on you
> and not on our own devices?
> Rule us and guide our prayer.

IX – Sacred Silence

Silent prayer in the presence of the Lord, speaking His NAME (YHWH), is indeed the sanctuary all must seek, and we must remain there as long as possible. For this is the union with God that is the end goal of every Christian soul.

Certainly one can be deluded and so must take care to keep oneself pure in the sight of God, as a loving child... but the fact that the soul so blessed with closeness to the Divine Lord may also be

Into Your Hands...

plagued with faults does not in itself mean it is deluded and led astray. The Lord can come as He pleases, even to the imperfect and to great sinners, to draw them unto Himself.

We should not judge the shortcomings of others, much less magnify them inordinately, or we may never find our path away from our own faults and into the Lord's presence.

> O Holy Spirit, always be our guide.
> Teach us to rely on you more and more,
> both to inspire our prayer
> and to understand the state of others,
> if it be our responsibility.
> Above all, let the Father's will be done –
> with Him let us become one.

X – YHWH

Is it not the holy NAME of God that is the divine interior and exterior silence every heart set aright desires? Is He not our natural center and does not speaking His NAME call us to Him? Is this not His great gift to those who pray, who seek Him? It is indeed a turning from creatures, from all created things.

The silence of our tongue and heart expresses, realizes, this turning away from the world, for it is a turning away from all words, except the Word Himself. O how the pure heart is irresistibly attracted to this divine silence, for in it we find our Creator.

> O Lord, let us sit with you as a child at your feet
> and hear your silence
> speak volumes to our heart.

Here in your presence we are at home;
here we taste Heaven.

XI – The Interior Spirit

To become mature in the faith and approach perfection, we must be guided peacefully by the Spirit of God – in Him we take our refuge regardless of the trials and troubles, or flattery, of the world. Suffering patiently any persecution will enable us to grow most quickly and perfectly. Certainly we must abide in faith and be detached from our feelings and desires, but it is being submissive in times of distress that will cause us to advance more so and become who the Lord created us to be. Let us learn to smile from the Cross.

We must work to diminish our faults, of course, but never in anxiety and always culling what grace and strength we can find in the humility they breed in us before God. Beg His forgiveness and know it is there as you rise once more as if nothing has happened.

Into what abyss of perversity we all would fall without the grace and guidance, without the peace that passes understanding that comes only from the Lord. Let us find that state wherein we are doing nothing yet everything, where we say nothing yet everything... where the Spirit speaks in us and works through us so perfectly, so imperceptibly, that we approach union with our God.

O Lord, let it be so
that your Spirit remain with us
to guide us within at all times.

XII – Heart of Peace

O to have always a peaceful heart, which is indeed the foundation of our interior life, for only by remaining in peace do we remain in God's presence – and if we are not in God's presence because of any anxiety or agitation of soul, we are certainly not where we must be.

Let us never be separated from Him and His holy will, which is to our advantage whatever trials or difficulties may come. These matter not. Let us but be resigned, completely resigned to His will, and we shall remain in peace, and we shall remain with Him.

But let us not become attached to any spiritual consolations the Lord may provide. These are not our end or goal but only the Lord Himself. Let us not be attached to them, nor to whatever distractions may arise. Let these latter but pass through; let them alone. Do not seek to grasp them or cast them out by force, for this will only mean their increase.

A simple glance of pure faith, a word to the Lord, calm in our soul... by this means we shall remain united to God as He ordains. In simplicity let us be with Him.

> Lord, breathe your peace into our hearts;
> unite us to you always.
> All we place in your hands
> that your will may be accomplished
> and we may join you in Heaven.

XIII – Our Misery

O what great grace it is to be in remembrance of our own misery, our own uselessness in the sight of

God, to realize that any good we do comes from Him alone; for it is He alone who could accomplish goodness in such wretched creatures as ourselves. This realization of our misery keeps us from becoming puffed up with pride, which would signal our greatest fall from grace into emptiness, into vanity, where God is not and we are left to our miserable selves.

By this means we are able to keep our peace before the Lord because by it we know there is nothing to take possession of in the gifts God provides – for they are indeed His gifts. And there is no need to fall into fear or anxiety regarding the ways we fall short of His glory, for we are what we are but He will save us if we give ourselves to Him. This is His great desire!

And so, let us sigh after God, let us raise our hearts to Him, and His presence shall never be far away.

> Lord, take from us all complacency and self-love
> that we might be blessed to be always
> at peace before you
> in a holy humility.

XIV – Detachment

Wonderful it is for the soul to receive divine favors, but we must always remember they will be followed by pains, by the dryness of the desert; and so we must always beware becoming attached even to the gifts that come only from God, for even these can distract us from God Himself. Let us but be docile before Him as He blesses us and allow Him to work as He will.

O to live only in Him! to desire only the silence and solitude that is His NAME... to find Him dwelling within our souls. We must renounce all that is not of Him and for Him, even innocent conversation, which, if let run, would take us from Him – even if we speak of Him! Let there be no obstacle to our union with the Lord.

> O Lord, help us to endure the agonies
> that must invariably come
> as we move closer to you
> and further from the world.
> Thank you for your sweet consolations
> along the way
> that enable us to go forward
> into the darkness
> that leads to the light of your Face.

XV – The Gift of God

If the Lord comes to us in our inmost sanctuary, speaking to our very heart with His blessed inspirations, we must accept this gift with humble gratitude and in all simplicity, without question or need for investigation, and His Spirit will form us into His likeness. Alleluia!

> O Lord, how wonderful it is when you deign
> to speak to us in our heart of hearts,
> when in silence you make yourself known;
> draw us ever closer to you by such graces
> and let us be one with you this day.

XVI – Enter the Darkness

Let us detach ourselves more and more from the world and from ourselves and allow God to work in our souls. Let us enter into His darkness; He is inaccessible to us, but by His grace and by our abandonment we may approach Him who is Light. The immensity of God we indeed cannot fathom, and how our heads spin in contemplating His majesty... but if we are able to suffer our own insignificance in patience and humility and without fear wait for Him to act upon us, He will come and bless our simple love for Him, for He indeed loves His children.

His martyrs of grace let us be, purified in peaceful waiting by the blessed pangs, the kisses of our Lord.

> O Lord, let us drink at the source
> which is you;
> let us be annihilated,
> utterly detached,
> that your love might fill us entirely.

XVII – The Spirit's Guidance

If we wish to make progress in the interior life, even unto intimate union with God in the innermost recesses of our spirit, then we must remain in peace and wait on Him to speak to us by the anointing of the Spirit that is upon our soul. Let us but desire to fulfill the divine will and we will be led to all the graces the Lord longs to shower upon us.

> O Lord, your voice is almost imperceptible
> to our poor senses,

and so, how quiet we must be
to hear the Spirit speak.
But if this is our desire and we persevere,
how greatly you will bless us
as the Spirit leads us to your light.

XVIII – Give Up Your Will

Let us submit ourselves to the Lord's holy will, which rules everything, even to the falling of a leaf from a tree. Our only rule should be the desires of God, and not our own.

Let us learn to have faith in Him even when He seems not to answer our prayers or be near us. In such darkness we find our trust in Him coming to perfection as we see the depths of our weakness and misery and how reliant we are on His grace. In such humility we find truth.

O to spend our whole lives in the silence of God, allowing the Holy Spirit to work on us! May we dwell with Him forever.

Lord, help us more and more
to give up our own will and desires
to embrace your will for our lives.
We are indeed miserable creatures –
breathe upon us the light of your grace.

XIX – The Single Desire

Why should we be concerned for any of the things of this world that but trouble our souls when in one moment, with one word, He can lead us forth better than even the well-meaning words of holy men. Let us but seek what He wishes to do with us and think of nothing else. Then we shall be at peace in His presence.

> O Lord, take the many distractions
> from our hearts and minds
> and focus us on your will alone –
> what more do we need?

XX – Empty Will

Let us find an emptiness of mind and will that the Lord may fill us with His presence, with His peace. Then we shall progress in the spiritual life. For our progress depends on the work of God (and not our own) and our submissiveness toward Him. We need but remain in silent humility accepting all as coming from His hand, and He will indeed bless us.

We must be as children, simple and true, indifferent to the world, our humble hearts set on God. Amen.

> O Lord, when we believe you are far away,
> it is then you are near,
> for it is then you work in our souls.
> Let us wish only what you wish
> and live in your love.

XXI – Let the Lord Act

Is it better we should act, or the Lord? Are the Holy Spirit's movements more beneficial, or our own? To pray formally is well and good, especially if the prayer flows freely and sincerely from our soul; but to sit in silence and allow the Lord to act in us and through us is more perfect, even as His works are above our own.

Turn to the Lord with an inclination of the heart, wait on Him with love... and when He comes and moves upon you, do not seek to leave His presence but surrender to Him all your time.

> Bless us, O Lord, with your Breath
> upon our souls,
> and let us sit and breathe with you.

XXII – Trust in God

O let us obey and please God in all things; let us hope against hope, knowing He can do all things and so can change night to day in a moment's time. What seems impossible to us is possible with Him – did not Mary trust in the Word spoken to her? Did not Abraham go as called?

We must have faith, brothers and sisters, or we have nothing at all; for without faith – and even its testing – we have not God, we know not God, who is all in all.

> Into your hands we commend our lives, O Lord,
> believing that your will is done
> in everything we undergo.

XXIII – The Desire

God looks upon the heart, certainly, and so our desire to serve Him, our love for Him, is what is most pleasing to Him. If we are ready and willing to sacrifice all for Him, then in a very real sense we have already done so. The rest is not up to us, and so we must leave the work He wishes for us to accomplish entirely to Him. We must never trust in ourselves or our own goodness but hope only in the goodness of God, ready to sacrifice even what we most desire (to serve Him), for this, too, is a blessed martyrdom.

> Lord, help us to open ourselves entirely
> to your will;
> give us the grace of readiness
> to sacrifice all for your sake,
> and we shall need nothing more.

XXIV – God's Power

By hidden but infallible means, indeed, the Lord accomplishes His will, even allowing His work to be thwarted that He might greater show His power. Has He not done this perfectly on the Cross? When all seems lost, when death is upon us, it is then He shows just how powerful He is – there is nothing that can stand in His way.

And so, let us remain in peace and seek always to subject our will to His, however dark things may seem.

> Only by serving you will we be happy, Lord;
> grant us the grace of perseverance
> in accepting your will
> that we might live by faith alone.

XXV – What God Wills

We should never will anything but what God wills; we should never be anxious when things do not go the way we expect or desire but humble ourselves in these moments and realize the hand of God is in them for our good.

If we desire something good, to make some sacrifice for the Lord, and it does not come to pass, it only means God is satisfied with our desire and does not require the sacrifice itself. And so we should be satisfied, too.

Be wise in the Lord and remain at peace, whatever the Lord may bring you.

> O Lord, help us to conform to your will
> and your way
> at all times.
> Take from us all self-love and self-will
> that indeed we might remain ever in your peace.

XXVI - Success

There is nothing that can stop the good, which is God's will, from succeeding; so we should entrust everything entirely into His hands, knowing that if our plans are thwarted, this too is for our good. Otherwise we shall know only anxiety and misery.

> All that is good succeeds in you, O Lord.
> May our trust in your will be complete
> and so we be at peace.

XXVII – Acceptance

What does it matter whether we are at prayer or working, whether we have this or that responsibility or not? If all is done for the love of God, then it is all the same. Let us be detached. Let us desire nothing nor refuse anything. Let us submit ourselves to God's holy will and the call of others and accept what comes to us. The Lord desires obedience, and if He calls us to some work we must go where He leads. We must be as useless servants.

> Let us not decide of ourselves
> what is for our good or not, dear Lord.
> Let us be indifferent about the work we must do,
> accepting all as in your holy will.

XXVIII – As God Wills

Each should follow where God leads and do what He ordains, whether it brings us peaceful repose or painful tribulation – the latter potentially being preferable for the graces that flow from our surrender.

Do all you can as God gives light... Eager for nothing, we shall be ready for anything.

> Lord, lead us where you will, as you will,
> and bless us with abandonment
> to your loving direction.

XXIX – The Present Moment

O to be like the spiritual master, abandoning ourselves completely to God, not knowing day to day where we will be or what we will do but having utter assurance that all will be well and that salvation awaits... for all is in the hand of God. This ignorance brings happiness, for we need be anxious about nothing nor concern ourselves with any decision: the Lord takes care.

O Lord, give us a taste of this sweet trust
in you and in your guidance,
that indeed we shall be like little children
simply looking up to you for everything.

XXX – Patience

How blessed are the sufferings we bear in patience, resigned to the will of God. They will be our Purgatory here on earth and so spare us from those greater pains. Let us be like Jesus on the Cross.

Any little faltering will not impede our path to the Lord if each day we give our 'fiat' to Him.

O Lord, let us be like Job, and greater than Job –
let us be like you on the Cross,
withholding complaint at the sufferings
that come.
Then your glory we shall also share.

XXXI – Death

Let us be ready always to give all back to God, who gives all things to us; let us be ready always even to die. Such sacrifice pleases our Father, who cannot be outdone in generosity.

Into your hands, O Lord,
I place all my life –
take what you will from me.

XXXII – Take Our Hearts

May the Lord indeed take our hearts, which long so for His love. May He overlook any small faults we commit against our neighbor, and may we stay on the straight road that leads to His divine love.

Bring us quickly into your Heart, O Lord.

XXXIII – Bearing Our Faults

We are but imperfect human beings – this we must accept. We cannot escape our faults, which we bear with us at all times; and so we should not be anxious about them but submit to God and put up with them in patience. And if our sorrow comes from a love of God and not ourselves, we will find great merit and progress in recognizing humbly how far short of His glory we fall.

O Lord, lead us to glory
by the acceptance of our faults
and your grace to overcome them.

XXXIV – Receiving Jesus

If we remain simple and humble, confident of the Lord's love and forgiveness, with a gentle and kind interior and exterior putting all things in His holy hands... then we shall be at peace as we approach the altar to receive our Divine Lord.

Let us come to you each day as you ordain,
O Lord our God;
write your Name upon our hearts
that we may remain always with you.

XXXV – Sanctifying Rest

Even our time of rest and recreation can be a means to sanctification if we raise our hearts and minds to God, setting aside all useless and anxious thoughts. Let us do all quietly and meditatively, offering any troubles to our Lord that they too might serve to transform us more and more into His image.

> O Lord, take our rest as well as our work,
> and make all conform to your holy will
> and be beneficial to our souls.

XXXVI – Blessed Chastisements

We should indeed make a sacrifice of all divine providence brings to us, and especially make holy use of sufferings; it will serve as great consolation on the day of eternity if we bear them well now, knowing they are all for our good in the will of the Lord. We shall then be as martyrs blessed by God for such humble sacrifice.

> O Lord, help us to bear our crosses lovingly
> and find in them the joy of knowing
> they have been arranged by you for our good.
> On this passing day,
> let our sights be set on eternal life.

XXXVII – No Consolations

Since the gifts of God are not God Himself, why should we seek consolation in them rather than the Lord? Do we not wish to be one with Him? Let us seek poverty then in spiritual as well as sensible things, having no attachment to them except insofar as they bring us to God. If the darkness we could bear, knowing the Lord is present even when He seems absent, how blessed we would be!

> O Lord, help us not to be attached
> to anything of this world
> but only to you, who are our God.

Third Book

I – Hidden Grace

Since we are miserable creatures, ever leaning into self-love and pride, since this is the truth of our existence, of ourselves, we must realize this truth, sink ourselves into this abyss, in order not to forget our unworthiness of the Lord's blessings, that we might be kept from that pride so ready to devour any progress we make toward the Lord of all. And so the graces the Lord works in us even as we admit our wretchedness, He keeps hidden from us, that we might continue to grow closer to Him and not fall into ourselves.

Ever must we be convicted of our misery, for ever we are ungrateful and unfaithful to our Lord, and then we will make progress toward Him. And it will be *His* glory alone we shall declare – the truth of His nature we also shall know! But till the day we die our misery must be foremost in our minds – though always in peace, always in *peace*; this is most important. (Never despair or become discouraged, even if you see not the progress you make.) Then His grace we shall know.

> O Lord, save us from all self-love;
> let us be formed in your holy image
> by repentance of our sin and weakness.
> Let us ever trust in you.

II – Divested of Pride

How hidden and persistent, and deadly, pride can be. How vain is the human inclined to become. How can he be healed except if the Lord punish him in His grace? And so He allows trials and temptations and takes from us what leads us into such self-love that we might know our weakness, our blindness, and our dependence on Him. How free the soul then becomes as it walks not with the devil and his evil but with the Lord and His goodness.

> O let us submit humbly to the bitter remedy
> you provide for our poor, forsaken souls, Lord!
> Give us the patience we need
> to remain childlike before you
> as you free us from all vain pride.

III – Restoring Peace

How important it is to maintain peace in our souls, and if we lose it, to gain it again and keep it close. For the Lord is peace and gives us His peace, and we must be good receivers of His peace.

If we are obedient as children to His voice speaking to us through the means He ordains, if we rest in Him and nurture quietness in our souls despite whatever temptations may come, and if we feed our souls with the spiritual nourishment of good books and holy conversation... then peace shall be ours, or return to us quickly when we stray.

Do not be anxious or afraid but trust in the Lord and accept all He wills for your life.

> O Lord, how easily the devil can lead us
> from your peace.
> Let us be as children upon your lap
> that we might be kept from all Satan's wiles.
> Return us ever to your presence.

IV – The Glory of God

We were created for the glory of God and to do His will, and so we should love first and foremost God in His glory and think of Him and His glory and not of ourselves. If we think of ourselves we will get lost in ourselves and become blind to the light of God. We must recognize our own misery – this is very important – but if we do not first abandon ourselves to God and His love, our perception of our faults and weaknesses will only make us anxious and afraid and draw us thus from the peace of the Lord. We must abandon ourselves to the glory of God and then we will see our misery in even clearer light, but with the consolation of our Lord. Then we shall approach the perfection of the saints, who were always most aware of their misery and whose awareness brought them closer to the Lord and made them confident of His love.

> O Lord, help us to turn from ourselves
> and toward you and your glory

that in the glory you ordain for us
we might stand,
miserable creatures that we are.

V – Sacrificing Affections

Must we not be like Abraham, who was willing to sacrifice his beloved son to the Lord at His command? We must place even those dearest to us in the hands of God, entrusting them and their future to Him. It does us no good to worry or think overmuch of them, even if they are in very difficult circumstances. We must raise ourselves above such feelings, knowing that even these pass like shadows, and make God our sole focus… for apart from Him nothing is real or lasting. He will take care.

O Lord, give us the wisdom and the grace
to entrust even your most precious gifts,
even those closest to us,
to you and to your providence.

VI – No Excuses

We must not excuse the attachments we allow ourselves or be distracted by foolish amusements but detach ourselves more and more, for only when our heart is empty of this world can God fill it with His love.

Forgive our weaknesses, O Lord;
make us strong in you.

Third Book

VII – Limiting Distractions

We should have as little intercourse with the world as reasonably possible and not be preoccupied with news from the outside. Even if not a religious, we should strive to remain as secluded and recollected as our station allows and see that we speak of God when communication is necessary. In this manner only will we progress in the spiritual life.

> Lord, help us keep our minds on you
> and on your Cross and Resurrection,
> for the edification of others as well as ourselves.

VIII – Excessive Activity

How lost we become when we submerge ourselves in excessive natural activity, which serves but to place confidence in ourselves rather than God. Our pride we puff up by our accomplishments... but is the Lord with us? This self-love must be torn up by its root and replaced with humility and self-distrust as we wait patiently for Him to act.

Even in our spiritual practices we should remain quiet and still, in peace as the Lord acts, even in remarkable ways, upon our soul. Never forget we deserve none of His graces and can do nothing on our own but turn to evil. And accept the afflictions He sends as blessings to purify us of our self-love.

> Lord, how inclined we are to complain,
> how inclined we are to hold on to our vanity –
> how attached we are to our own works.
> Let us come rather to you
> and do only as you desire.

IX – Calm

Calm we must remain even in our most saintly desires.

Let us keep ever in your peace, O Lord.

X – Recollection

All things should lead to recollection and the development of a spirit of recollection that our souls may be set ever on God when we read – as when we do all things – so the words may sink deeply into our hearts and bear fruit. It is not the number of words we read that matters but the depth of recollection we find.

O Lord, let us be united to you in all we do
as your simple children.

XI – Correction

How much we must beware of the way we correct others! Though we may be right in what we say, if we do not say it with love but with any bitterness at all, it is best we keep our mouth shut until we can speak with all humility and no condemnation. We must be patient and understanding with the faults of others, with a true concern for their welfare… and at the same time empty ourselves of any vain superiority. Let us rather think of our own faults and their gravity before our holy Lord. This should humble us before any sin of another and produce kindness and charity toward them. If it does not, we are lost.

O Lord, teach us how to speak;
let the plank be removed from our own eye
that we may sincerely be of assistance
to others.

XII – Obedience

How important is obedience, and yet how lacking, in those who break the commands of God, yes, but also in those who presume their own will is the will of the Lord. The Lord has said, "I desire obedience more than sacrifice," and so we should not be attached to our sacrifices, especially not putting them before obedience to superiors. This is what will truly make us holy, free of self-love. For indeed the Lord delights not in sacrifices themselves but in our following His will. And if the Lord delights in us, what more do we need?

O Lord, help us to sacrifice our will
and follow your word and your way
as it comes to us through those you send,
that the delights of Heaven might be our own.

XIII – Little Children

Be as the weakest and least of all. Only as a child do we enter the Kingdom; obedient let us ever be, humble before our Lord and others.

How subtle and insidious pride can be, and so, how we must be ever on our guard against it, renouncing our will in all things. For if we follow our own ideas, it will not be an image of the Lord we become but an image of ourselves, and what a horror that would be.

O Lord, let us be free of self-love;
let us take no pleasure in the admiration of others
but seek only and always your approval
by remaining simple as a child at your feet,
ready to do your will.

XIV – Disclosure of Faults

How necessary it is to openly disclose one's faults, to bring them into the light, especially in Confession. If we hide them from the priest or reason them away, they will only fester and bring more darkness to our souls.

Even the speaking of others against our faults we should welcome, as this serves their cleansing by the light as well. But let us always think of ourselves, of our own sins, and not the sins of others.

O Lord, grant us such openness
to admit our faults,
that you may quickly heal them.

XV – The Use of Faults

We should not be discouraged by our faults, becoming anxious and approaching the despair the devil devises, but realize the opportunity the Lord provides for us to gain greater humility by the recognition of our weakness. In peace let us accept our faltering, and in picking ourselves up again we shall find renewed confidence and commitment to the will of God. In this way we grow closer to Him.

> Lord, how great you are, how powerful!
> that even our faults can be used by you
> to bring about our greater good.

XVI – False Fears

Show confidence in the face of the false fear by which the devil tempts your soul as it seeks perfection in Christ. We must not allow vexation or depression to take hold of us but remember always the grace of the Lord and turn to Him giving all over to Him, taking refuge in His words and His ways rather than the ways of the world.

Others may mock us and try to guide us away from the conviction and total self-giving to which we are called. But be not concerned for false human respect; listen rather to God's call. Find His humility in your soul even by means of the false fears that tempt you. God uses them for good, to prepare you to receive His gifts and graces without the poison of pride or self-love.

What seems difficult now will become as natural to you when time has passed and your soul has been readied to receive His grace. Then you will walk freely in His light and shine that light to others.

> O Lord, let us not be afraid
> of the mockery of the world
> or our own weakness
> but come to you as you call
> and by patience find you living within us.

Into Your Hands...

Fourth Book

I – Green Wood

How the soul that longs for God but is not yet perfect is like green wood tossed into the fire – with what twists and turns and great noise it is made dry for burning! And so we must suffer with patience the trials that come to us because of our self-love, because of our need to be purified of our willfulness and submit to the will of God.

But the pains we undergo, even the temptations we experience, we must see as a blessing from the Lord, and love them, accepting them patiently, quietly, as they rain down from His hand to purge us of all the weakness that necessitates them. Let us bow humbly under the mighty hand of God, whatever we must suffer, and thank Him for all that comes to us. Forward let us travel, trusting in His silence.

> O Lord, there is nothing more pleasing to you
> than a broken and humble heart.
> Help us to welcome the crosses we must bear
> to enter into your presence.
> In peace let us remain
> despite the surrounding troubles.

II – Light and Darkness

Both trials and consolations come from the hand of God for the benefit of our souls, and both are indispensible. We must learn that the Lord bestows His favors where and when He will and that they do not come by our own industry. All vestiges of self-love must be taken from us, and so we should welcome trials most, since they bring its destruction.

> O Lord, let us remain patient under trials
> and find your blessed hand at work in them
> for our purification.

III – A Suffering Peace

Even in violent afflictions of soul we must find the peace of the Lord by submitting entirely to His will, that by such sacrifice our self-will may be purged and we may live in His grace alone. If we have such confidence in Him even in the deepest darkness, the greatest blessings we shall know as all cruel tyrants are cast to the ground.

> Lord, is there a greater peace in this world
> than the one you knew on the Cross
> as you submitted yourself to the Father's will?
> Help us find that peace.

IV – The Dark Dungeon

What afflictions we must suffer in order to find total distrust of ourselves and complete trust in God. But even in the darkest dungeon, even amid paroxysms of pain that seem to consume us, we must be obedient and remain in peace, holding on to the hope that we will see the blessings that come from such humiliation; for indeed by this suffering we are cured of self-love.

> We know more progress is made
> in suffering than in action, O Lord,

but how hard it is to remember
when in its throes!
Help us to endure all afflictions
with patient trust in you.

V - The Dark Night

In the darkening of the senses is found the light of the Spirit. All sensible consolation must be taken from us if we are to find pure faith in God and no trust at all in ourselves and our feelings. Great is the value of this purity, of this dark night of the senses and of the spirit – therein our love of God may become pure, and we may worship the Lord in spirit and in truth, in the simple prayer of the heart. God sees all things – keep your will fixed on Him and you will see with Him.

O Lord, take from us all that is not you;
let us not be deceived by passing feelings
or put our trust in them.
You alone are God
and wish to draw us to yourself –
empty of all else,
let us be filled with your presence
in the essence of our souls.

VI – Being with God

We are most blessed when we simply sit, simply pray in the presence of God, in silence, with trust in His holy will for us. This is not a waste of time, except to the world, which would draw us from Him. And so let us accept, let us cherish this blessing, whatever doubts or fears may come,

Fourth Book

whatever stupidity we may seem to possess in the eyes of others.

> O Lord, help us to abandon ourselves
> entirely to you,
> seeking only your will and your presence,
> and all else that is good shall follow.

VII – In Weakness

We should accept and embrace our weakness, for such recognition is a blessing from the Lord. It is in weakness that we are strong, for it is indeed weak instruments that God uses to exalt His glory.

And so, remain patient in humiliations; fret not over your lack of consolation. It is the will of God that must be accepted, whatever that will may be – this is what matters. Live in solitude and silence as His humble child, and you will find the union with Him you seek.

> O Lord, help us to be detached from all things,
> especially our own will and judgment.
> Let us accept all our weakness
> and know that you will make us strong,
> able thus to do your will.

VIII – No Pleasure

We should not seek pleasure or sensible consolations in prayer, or think that without them our prayers are useless… We must accept the lack of feeling and even embrace it as a gift from the Lord, if for nothing else to bring us to a greater humility and a purer faith.

It is pure faith that should be our goal, and so even involuntary distractions should be borne with patience as we keep our hearts set on this goal. Keep your prayer simple, and quiet your soul.

O Lord, help us to pray to you faithfully,
expecting nothing in return.

IX – Poor in Spirit

When the Lord withdraws His sensible presence, when we feel the absence of God, how our soul rebels – how it falls into fear and anxiety as the darkness comes upon us! But we must be made pliant to the movements of the Holy Spirit, and so such deprivation is necessary. It is by this poverty we are drawn closer to God and away from ourselves; we need but submit to it.

Lord, help us overcome our mortal nature,
which stands in opposition to your immortal call.
Help us empty ourselves entirely
that we might be filled with your joy.

X – Inner Chamber

God dwells in the inner chamber of our hearts, hidden deep within our souls as in an abyss, and we can only know Him by profound recollection and by the effects He works in us. But all we need is this dry peace and the quiet sadness it brings to be assured of His presence. And all we need do is praise Him in any tribulations that may come from our apparent separation from Him, and we will be consoled even in the deepest darkness.

Lord, how hidden you are.
And if we but accept your hiddenness,
you become known to us.
Praise you!

XI – Holy Self-Contempt

It is simply true that we can do nothing for God and whatever we attempt is spoiled by our self-love; thus is the Lord pleased when we are displeased with ourselves, when we humble ourselves in a holy self-contempt. This self-contempt is holy because, first of all, it is the truth; but also because it gains the Lord's sympathy for our poor souls and so brings His graces upon us.

Hating ourselves and our sins and weakness, we learn to hope only in Him who is all Truth itself.

O Lord, make us ready to know the truth
and to remember it:
that we are nothing but inclined to sin
and you are all Goodness, our salvation.
Help us to believe in your grace,
even if we do not see it or feel it.

XII – Days of Agony

Privations and suffering, profound spiritual darkness – what should this resemblance to our Crucified Savior bring us but a certain joy, knowing there is a light that shines even in these times? For our Risen Lord and our Crucified Lord are indeed one, and that light will soon shine brightly.

Ask for no more pain than the Lord gives, and accept the consolation He provides... Find no troubles even in the suffering and you will be on the road to God.

> In this world what better can we do
> than to suffer with you, dear Jesus?
> Help us discover the grace
> such sharing in your Cross is for our souls
> and those of others.

XIII – Desire to Pray

The Lord looks upon the heart and the will and He lives in the higher realms of the soul, and so if we are unable to express our desires or if troubles surround us, these things are not what is consequential: we must but have the sincere desire to offer ourselves to the Lord in complete submission and He will be pleased more than if we speak the greatest prayer. And should there be distractions in the lower portion of our soul, in the sensible realm, if we can maintain peace in the higher part, these troubles will be opportunities to share in the sufferings of Christ and so prove meritorious for us.

> O Lord, let our hearts be set upon you
> that we may always be with you
> where you are.

XIV – Accepting Suffering

God gives to all as He pleases and what He pleases, and we can be assured that our loving Father does always as is best for us. Thus whether we receive consolations or sufferings, they should all be accepted as from His hand.

Fourth Book

And the way of suffering is indeed the more blessed path, if only we could realize this, if only we could see the graces He has stored up for those who are crucified with Him. Let us but believe this, let us but submit to that which the Lord gives us, and find joy and praise for His hand upon us.

> Bless those who suffer
> with knowledge of you, Lord;
> let them understand it is indeed a blessing
> from your hand.
> Help us to see with your eyes
> and your heart
> your wounds upon us.

XV – Listen to Him

There is nothing more valuable, more worthy of our time and attention, than peaceful repose in the presence of the Lord. Let us not get caught up in thinking and talking and acting... Though we must think and talk and act, let us always do so with Jesus at heart and be led from this place – let us never be afraid to pause, to stop all thinking and talking and doing simply to be in His presence. Only then can we listen to Him, only then can we hear His voice and be directed on right paths to His glory, which is all we ought to desire.

> O Lord, help us set aside
> all the things of the world
> that our hearts might be set on you alone
> and we might hear your voice
> in the silence.

XVI – Antidote to Pride

We cannot be filled with the Spirit of God until we have been emptied of self, and so we must endure the humiliations that serve to purge us of self-love. We must submit to the state of nothingness, accept our own miseries, and the Lord will be permitted to work in our souls.

With Christ let us remain in the Garden of Olives, let us find a holy love of self-abnegation, and we will make progress toward our Divine Spouse.

> O Lord, take all vanity and pride from us
> by the means you know is best –
> into your silence let us come
> and there make our home.

XVII – Nothing in Ourselves

O let us die to ourselves! Let us know we have done nothing, that we can do nothing – that there is no merit in ourselves – and so draw closer to God, closer to the truth of our own misery and the glory of the Lord. Let us rather be afflicted and suffer many difficulties than fall into any semblance of self-love; let us be purified of such inclination and put our faith in God alone. In such submission let us find our joy.

> O Lord, how can we come to the knowledge
> that we are nothing
> and you are all that is Good?
> Deprive us of all sensible graces
> till with cleansed vision we look upon you alone.

XVIII – Salutary Bitterness

Let our nature revolt and our pride be humiliated – this is good for our souls; this is the medicine we most need to cure us of self-love. In such sacrifice we find union with the will of God, for all that is earthly and illusory is thus taken from us and all we have left is a pure faith, which alone will sustain us.

Let us abandon ourselves in confidence to God and only fear offending Him.

> O Lord, you make sweet the most bitter trials;
> you console us in our afflictions
> with the touch of your sacrificial love.
> And we are joined to you.
> Increase this grace in us.

XIX – Mercy in Punishment

Whatever sufferings we undergo, even if they be punishment for our faults, may serve to purify our souls and bring us closer to the Lord, by His grace and mercy. The Lord does nothing except out of love and to draw us closer to His love, and so even His chastisements are wrought with His grace and bring blessed mercy to our souls. Though no man should ever sin and sin is always loathsome in God's sight, He can turn even sin into an opportunity for grace. And so we should never despair, for His love never ends.

> O Lord, your chastising hand brings your justice,
> helping us atone for our sins,
> and the sufferings we undergo thereby
> may be a blessing, purifying our souls.
> Let it be so.

XX – Profound Peace

O what a blessing of the Holy Spirit it is to know profound inner peace in quiet recollection as we remain simply and humbly in the presence of God. There is nothing on earth more wonderful – it is our hope, for it is a sign we are with Him. And so, why should we care about whatever trials or deprivations we suffer to find our way there?

> O Lord, let us be filled with your peace
> and remain in your presence
> forever.

XXI – Fruit of the Cross

Let us not be afraid to face the collection of miseries that is our true self, that we might find the glory of God in their purgation from our souls. For looking upon such horror, what sin, what pride, could survive? And so we should welcome the pain the Lord grants us to achieve the grace of being made pure in His sight. Let us rejoice in the goodness of God even as we mourn our own misery.

> O Lord, help us to suffer well
> the pain that brings such blessed consolation;
> recognizing our guilt before you,
> may we come to eternal life.

Fifth Book

I – Feebly Suffering

When we are without strength or courage, humbled and confounded before God by our weakness, yet suffer our sickness peacefully and patiently, even thanking the Lord for such opportunity to realize our feebleness… this is a great grace, a great blessing from our God. For then we know who we are, and depend upon Him alone.

> O Lord, sanctify us
> by the realization of our littleness;
> may we be always obedient,
> accepting the trials that come to us
> as the weak human beings we are.

II – Little Crosses

How big we make the little crosses the Lord provides day to day for our salvation, for how easily we are troubled by them and fall into complaint and distraction instead of bearing them well and finding the grace and consolation they bring. How foolish we are to be so blind to the Lord's providence – rather, let us submit ourselves to the crosses and so be blessed.

> O Lord, we say we want to follow you,
> yet against even the slightest cross we rebel.
> Help us to overcome our weak nature
> and unite ourselves to you
> and your blood.

III – Blessed Disasters

Even the terrible disasters that befall us or our society may be seen as sent by God to serve our detachment from the world and thus our salvation – we must see even these as blessings. For indeed, even the anger of the Lord comes from His mercy, from His desire for us to be in loving union with Him. Let us always give our 'fiat' to the will of God and so find His peace.

> O Lord, your glory is so great
> that even the worst disasters
> you turn to our good,
> as you have done with the Cross.

IV – True Charity

If we must endure those who particularly disgust us, this is opportunity to practice true charity, for even the pagans love those who love them. Is it not our call to love our enemies? Is this not our greatest blessing? Let us live as we should, loving all.

> O Lord, grant us such patience and gratitude
> that we may receive the graces
> that come from true charity.
> Thank you for your mercy.

V – Occasions for Patience

How little things and people in our daily lives can try our patience! But how blessed we are to have these small crosses. For it is indeed by these that great graces may come; by faithfulness under these trials we will find the gift of interior peace and prayer.

Remember that we must forgive others as God has forgiven us and these occasions for grace will not seem so difficult.

> Lord, help us to see as you see,
> to be as you are –
> help us to find your patient love,
> especially for those who most trouble us.

VI – Everything Is from God

How greatly we would benefit if we could but believe this truth: that everything but sin comes from God and is in His holy will. We would then save ourselves from torturous rebellion against that which pains us in this life. Even the consequences of sin and the afflictions produced thereby are in His will to purge us from self-love and bring us to Heaven. And so, let us accept and submit to any persecution or humiliation and not allow the devil to make us uneasy therein.

> O Lord, this truth so easily escapes us
> as we seek to escape from trials –
> help us in joy to embrace your Cross!

VII – Domestic Difficulties

Indeed, the constant friction of living with those of a different character can be a most difficult task, especially when we suffer injustice at their hands. We want to cry out like Job of our innocence and call on remedy from the Lord. But what do we do when

He is silent? We must be like Christ and bear the Cross, and be silent ourselves.

> Lord, give us your patience
> that when we suffer great torment
> we might not torment ourselves
> but offer everything over to you and your will.

VIII – Prayer of Confidence

Let us confide in God all our troubles and afflictions, knowing that He hears and has the most sympathetic ear, and all will be easier to bear and our merit will be so much the greater than if we complain to anyone else. This will best benefit our detachment from others and the world.

> Lord, let us come to you in faith,
> pouring out our hearts before you,
> and all our needs will be fulfilled
> and we will draw closer to you.

IX – Sharing the Chalice

Let us take our daily wounds, as repeated and unjust as they may be, and offer them back to the Lord through whom they come, avoiding all bitterness as we forgive those who harm us and pray God's graces upon them. Then we shall be sharing in the chalice of our Savior.

> O Lord, help us to endure any torment
> as you did on the Cross.
> Enable us to share in your Blood.

X – By Divine Judgment

If we judge things by human standards, with our weak and narrow minds, we will never come to understand our Lord and Savior and His way to Heaven – we will never enter the spiritual life He prepares for us. We will remain blind to the gifts and graces that come with the Cross.

> O Lord, help us to see as you see
> and so to be as you are,
> lest we fail to grasp the hand
> you reach down to us
> to draw us from the choppy sea.

XI – On Him Alone

If we find ourselves abandoned by all of this world, what a joy this should be for us, for what do we need but God alone; and so to come to the place where we must depend on Him alone should be seen as a great grace. Let life be sad, let terror come to our souls as death nears… It is all from the Spirit of God as He draws us unto Himself.

> O Lord, accomplish your desire
> to free us from all attachment to this world
> that we might be attached to you alone,
> whatever the cost.

XII – Only God

With no other support it will seem as if we are alone and lost… but it is then we must trust only in God; and so we are never alone, for He is omnipresent and always concerned for us. He will direct us if we but trust in Him.

> What more do we need than you, O Lord?
> And knowing this, how blessed we are!
> It is then we find true joy.

XIII – Sole Confidence

The Lord desires all our confidence be in Him, for He is jealous of us and of our love. And so, should we not give it entirely to Him? Should we be concerned when anything that is not Him is taken from us? How shall we come to see that He is all we need?

> Take all attachments from us, Lord;
> help us realize the salutary nature
> of the pain we know thereby.
> For it is you to whom we thus come.

XIV – Merciful Punishment

How much better to suffer now the deprivation of all worldly attachments than to suffer such detachment in Purgatory, where the pain is so much more severe. How blessed we are to be gradually deprived of everything while still on this earth; and so let us give our ready 'fiat' to the Lord and the work He accomplishes in us, thereby uniting ourselves with Him alone.

> To Heaven let us come, O Lord,
> even as we crawl upon this earth.
> Beyond the crucifix lies our eternal happiness.

XV – Blessed Ignorance

It is so, that spiritual progress is made by means of troubles, and the greatest progress is made when we are unaware of its workings. When we believe all is going wrong, that we are quite lost, it is then the Lord is working in our soul to draw it unto Himself. If we can but unite our will to His in these times, what grace will be ours! Though His gradual working in our soul may be imperceptible to us – a grace in itself (lest we spoil all) – it is very sure nonetheless. Praise God!

> Lord, give us the humility and trust
> and patience we need
> to find your good will at work in our souls
> in the trials we undergo,
> that we might come quickly to you.

XVI – Happy Privations

Let us be tranquil and happy in the face of bitter disappointments, and even death will become sweet to us as we find the hand of the Lord at work for our good in all these privations.

> O Lord, may everything serve our sanctification
> as we give our 'fiat' to your holy will,
> whatever the circumstances may be.

XVII – Providential Pains

The chalice from which we must drink in this world can be bitter, but how much more bitter the chalice drunk in Hell or Purgatory! And so, the sufferings we find in this life can truly be said to be providential, to be for our own good, for if we bear them patiently, our souls will make great progress and the pains of the afterlife we will avoid.

> Lord, help us to accept the suffering you send
> to purify our souls
> and not try to make our own way
> through this world.

XVIII – Pitiful Blindness

Why do we trouble ourselves by worrying about things that may never happen or seek to effect our own will and desires when it is only in submission to the will of God we find peace? It is perfect foolishness. Even if His will brings difficulties (or if we continue to bring them upon ourselves by our useless worrying), still we can find the peace of the Lord by accepting all as coming from His hand and returning to Him.

> O Lord, how pitiable indeed we are
> in our blind desires
> and in tormenting ourselves with worry –
> into your hands let us commend our lives.

XIX – Submission to Chastisement

Knowing that all passes but God remains, let us submit ourselves to His holy will, suffering patiently and with the expectation of glory all the chastisements that come to us as individuals or as a people. Truly, His punishment is oriented toward our salvation.

Thank you, Lord, for all that comes to us
by your chastising hand.
You desire only our union with you.

Sixth Book

I – The Horror of Sin

The more we fear offending the Lord, the more we can be assured we have not consented to temptations; and the greater our anguish, the more merit we obtain. Though this be a great trial, though the temptations strike fear in us, we must trust in the Lord and His great love, which will never allow us to be separated from Him against our will.

O Lord, let us never offend you;
lead us not into temptation –
keep us ever free from evil.

II – Spiritual Battle

Unending is our battle for Christ and against all temptations: this is our call in this life. And so we should embrace the struggle against the world, the flesh, and the devil, knowing who fights for us and so having utter confidence in our victory. Let us not be cowards; let us not fear faltering in the field of battle but trust in the goodness of our God and His power to turn even our weaknesses into opportunities for greater grace.

Into Your Hands...

> Be with us, O Lord, in all our struggles;
> help us to trust in you.
> If you fight for us, who can defeat us?
> Let us be your foot soldiers in this world.

III – The Way of Pure Faith

How dark is the path faith must walk, yet it is the way that leads to light; and so, how surely we must walk it. And if we remember that through all trials and temptations the Lord is leading us to empty ourselves that we might be filled with His light, if we have faith in the light coming to us despite the darkness that surrounds us... how blessed will this path be, for it is the path to joy.

Fear not the humiliation you suffer, the misery you see in yourself, for it is true we are but miserable creatures – the devil is not wrong in the accusations he hurls at us. But know, too, the truth of God's mercy and goodness; remember that though we are but nothing, in Him we find all things, and you will defeat the devil at his own game... for his temptations will be turned to means of embracing our surrender to the Lord, who is our life.

> Help us, Lord, to see through the darkness,
> to be so strong in faith
> that the darkness we might drink in without fear
> as we become one with your light.
> May we find our peace in you alone.

IV – Advantageous Grief

Let us accept everything as coming from the hand of God and even the most difficult trials will gain us grace in the end. If humbled before the Lord we will be purified of all self-seeking by what we suffer. We must will what pleases God and in His good pleasure we will find our perfection.

> Forgive us, O Lord, all our transgressions,
> all our doubts and fears;
> let us see your will done in all things.

V – Salutary Trouble

The suffering we undergo is a sign of God's mercy, for by it He purifies our souls.

We should not be distressed by the troubles we find in the inferior part of our soul, over which we have little control; or rather, we should not be distressed by the distress itself, for the sadness we feel at the thought of not submitting ourselves wholly to the will of God is proof we desire such submission, and so, that it is present in the superior part of our soul, which is what matters.

Let our self-love be destroyed by the troubles – this is the grace we need. Simply be confident that the Lord remains present, though hidden, as He draws us closer to His presence.

> Into your hands, O Lord, we commend our spirit.

VI – Waiting under Shelter

It is God's will we depend entirely upon Him, and so when all sensible sweetness is taken from our souls and we are left with only pain and distress, let us be patient and wait. It is by this means the Lord purifies us of all self-love, and so this state should not make us anxious or upset but should be recognized as an opportunity to trust in Him, to find greater faith. And so, offer up the darkness and deprivation for the salvation of souls, especially your own. The storm will soon pass.

> Thank you, Lord, for your gracious concern
> for the state of our souls;
> teach us the patient endurance
> that leads to union with you.

VII – Fortunate Weakness

How we should rejoice as the Lord takes more and more of our power and our understanding from us and leaves us in a kind of despair for our inability to love and serve Him well – let us abandon even our abandonment and then perfection will be upon us!

How blessed is spiritual poverty, the realization that we can do nothing, that we are nothing… for then we may come to know the transcendent Lord, who seems like nothing Himself but is indeed all things and calls us unto Himself.

> O Lord, let us simply desire you,
> and rejoice even if this desire we do not see –
> it is then you who are invisible
> may become known to us.

VIII – Salutary Blindness

Our want of sensible tenderness for God should not trouble us but should rather be endured in peace, and it will become a source of grace. As long as we work to diminish such miseries, the Lord knows and understands, for He sees what He keeps hidden from our eyes (lest we fall into a dangerous pride): that we still possess true love of Him in the apex of our souls.

> O Lord, teach us to love you the more dearly
> the more blind we are to your presence –
> by faith let us know your grace at work in us.

IX – Follies of the Imagination

Let us not terrify ourselves by idle thoughts and imaginings, unaware of how seasons change and the weather varies. Remain still and in peace – do not move with your imagination but drop such thoughts like a rock. Let the vicissitudes be. Do not anxiously chase these flies.

But for whatever pain does come by them, rejoice for the fruit derived from suffering in patience any trial.

> O Lord, help us to appreciate all your gifts,
> be they in fair or foul weather;
> in you we find our sturdy shelter.

X – Invisible Works

We should not be discouraged or disheartened at our weakness and misery, nor compound our troubles by troubling about them; rather, let us remain tranquil, trusting in the Lord, remembering that all our crosses come from Him for our sanctification. That sanctification is occurring in our souls (though we may be unaware of its operations) if we but maintain our holy desire for God and all that leads to Him... and rise gently from our falls.

O Lord, keep our hearts fixed on you
that all may be for our good,
as dark as things may seem.

XI – Be at Peace

Do not dwell on the torments that interior crosses bring but be submissive and resigned to them. Rid yourself of sin as best you can and trust in the Lord's grace and forgiveness. Endure patiently the troubles that come and blessings will follow.

Lord, help us to be at peace in your presence
despite the troubles we undergo.
Help us to seek and to trust in your forgiveness.

XII – Contrite Confession

Do not doubt at all the graces conferred by the priest in the sacrament of Confession. Remember your horror for sin and that you would never sin mortally, never separate yourself from the mercy of God, and accept the penance the priest provides to wash clean the sins upon your soul.

Lord, help us to have faith in your mercy
and to see that our hearts desire to be clean.

XIII – Inevitable Vicissitudes

We cannot feel the imperceptible nor find a certainty that is beyond this life, and so we should not be concerned at being on fire at one time and cold as ice another but resign ourselves to the gifts God provides, especially treasuring those most above the senses and most mortifying to our self-love.

Into your hands, Lord, we commend our senses.

XIV – Certainty in Doubt

We must abandon ourselves to the mercy of God to be assured of our salvation. Though we see nothing but poverty and misery in ourselves and can never be certain of our place with the Lord, if we annihilate ourselves before Him and present all our miseries to Him, His mercy will be ours, and in His mercy is our salvation.

Lord, help us to be assured of your grace
upon miserable souls.

XV – Sincere Desire

If we truly desire to confess all our sins, then we should believe that the Lord hears us and forgives. In any of our shortcomings we should humbly lament our state and desire to be lifted up, and our prayer will be answered sooner or later. All that matters is that we know, love, and serve God.

O Lord, look upon our weakness
and hear our hearts cry out to you.
In your mercy, you will bless us.

XVI – Sweet Tears

Our holiness does not consist in the works we do or how we feel but in our humility and the sacrifice of our lives to the will of God. And so God will keep us from falling into self-love by hiding His graces from us that we might not grow proud; and so it is only our own misery we can see. But this abjection should lead us, as it has the saints, to greater and greater humility, and so, greater and greater sanctity. In the tears for our sins let us ever maintain a certain cheerfulness before the Lord, remembering the work He is doing in our souls.

> O Lord, prepare us more and more
> for union with you
> in the way you know is best for us,
> in our spiritual poverty.
> For this we praise you.

XVII – Avoid Distress

Since the devil fishes in troubled waters, we should make it a priority to avoid distress and discouragement regarding our weaknesses and the humiliations that come to us; we should rather treasure humility and the grace it brings in freeing us from self-love, and remain ever in peace. And remember, the greater the battle, the greater the victory.

> Lord, help us not to grow anxious
> when suffering comes
> but to endure all in patience and in peace,
> knowing you are at work in our souls
> for our greater glory.

XVIII – Patient Impatience

All is in God's hands, and so why should we fear? We must but place ourselves in His hands, enduring all the trials that come to us and knowing that these crosses are the path to salvation; for has our Savior not trod the same road?

> Help us not to fear, Lord,
> nor to be impatient with our weakness;
> help us to embrace your Cross
> and therein find our salvation.

XIX – Humble Yourself

How wonderful it is to humble ourselves before God! To remain humble is to remain with God, in His peace. Then even our faults become opportunity to increase in virtue, to draw closer to the Lord. Here is cause for rejoicing!

Self-love mixes with everything and must be extinguished from our souls. If we see it in others, let us make excuse for them; and let us always be on guard against it in ourselves.

> O Lord, keep us humble,
> humble as you were upon the Cross;
> then we shall be free –
> then we shall become one with Thee.

XX – Treasure Poverty

What a blessing it is to become more and more convinced that we are miserable creatures, to draw ever closer to the light of the Lord and so see ever more clearly our faults and failings. Though we must always work to rid ourselves of our imperfections, the recognition of our poverty should bring us great joy – for then we can indeed draw closer to God.

> O Lord, help us to love our enemies,
> to pray for those who persecute us…
> to accept in peace and seek to remedy
> all the emptiness we find in ourselves.

XXI – Silence in Agony

We are nearest the Lord when we suffer; let us suffer as He did, in silence, and great will be our reward, for we will be like Him. The Father will sustain us as He has His Son – but desire His will in the higher part of your soul and His grace and peace shall be with you.

> Help us, O Lord, to accept the Father's will
> as you did,
> without complaint, with humble submission,
> that our sufferings may be as sanctified.

XXII – Avoid Bitterness

We must be gentle with ourselves as we should always be with others when correction is necessary. We must not fall into trouble or by a false humility torment ourselves but trust in the Lord and turn to Him as a child, seeking His help and direction – it will certainly be present to save us. All chastisement should be accepted in silence as a deserved punishment as we place ourselves in the hand of our Judge with confidence in His grace.

> Teach us, O Lord, to be gentle as you,
> that true progress will be made
> in our spiritual lives
> by tranquil repentance of our sins.

XXIII – Happy Humiliation

When the sorrow's so deep you feel nothing but joy, then you will know the humbled are exalted. When you have realized fully the depths of your nothingness, then the Lord will fill you with His Spirit, raising you to His heights.

But it is nothing you can attain on your own; indeed, you must be emptied of anything that is of the world, you must trust in Him alone... then the truth and life and joy of His presence will be with you, and nothing else will you need.

> O Lord, how you support us in our weakness!
> How you raise us by your grace from our misery!
> Let your will be done in our lives.

XXIV – Fortunate Trials

If we can but accept the humiliations that come to us by our trials and troubles and even our faults, spiritual progress we shall make – and for this we should thank the Lord.

> Lord, help us remain in peace under trial
> and torture,
> and we will know how salutary it is
> to be submissive to your holy will.

XXV – The Foot of the Cross

In silence let us remain at the foot of the Cross when troubles come upon us. Let us offer them up to the Father and say with the Son, "Let Thy will be done." Let us not be anxious or practice vain scruples but remain in peace, for peace comes from God. The rest let us simply endure.

> At the foot of the Cross
> let us make our home, Lord,
> when the troubles of this world come upon us.
> By our endurance may our souls be purified
> for your Kingdom.

XXVI – Bare Faith

It is having but a simple ray of faith, a faith which seems like darkness, that is most meritorious for our souls; for if we rely on sensible pleasure, how deep is our union with the Lord? It is but His comforts we then desire and not He Himself. It is the Cross that unites us to Him.

We should embrace every humiliation that comes to us, for God offers them that they might kill our self-love and keep us from falling back upon our own ways.

> Lord, help us to embrace abjection
> that by this darkness we might find
> the light of faith hidden from our eyes.

Seventh Book

I – A Block of Wood

The state of darkness, of deprivation of all that is sensible, is indeed a great gift from the Lord; and into His hands as the great Physician we should thus place ourselves, trusting in nothing but His mercy even as we lie on our death bed. Remember, what is most bitter is most sanctifying, and so we would thank the Lord for this great grace if we could but see His hand at work. Let us be pleased as we can by this annihilation of our self-love.

> O Lord, into your hands we commend our lives,
> trusting in you like a block of wood
> under your purifying touch.

II – Blind Obedience

Walking by the light of blind obedience to the will of God and the guidance of His representatives is the surest path to glory. Though crucifying it may be, it thus serves better to keep us from the distracting light of sensible pleasure, and so, self-love.

> O Lord, help us to die to self
> that we might live with you;
> let us not be afraid of the darkness
> that leads us to you.

III – Crushing Weight

We must accept any crushing weight upon our spirits as coming from the hand of the Lord – in it is unimaginable grace. In it is the Cross, in it is blessed penance... let us with courage abandon ourselves to the will of God.

> Help us be obedient
> to all that you will, O Lord,
> enduring every trial with trust in your goodness
> and grace.

IV – Longing for God

The hunger and thirst of the soul can only be satisfied by heavenly food, by God Himself, and we must desire Him ardently in order to possess His love. This love may be crucifying, yes, as we are bereft of all that is not God... but soon we shall burn brightly and eternally in His presence.

> May your fire burn away the green wood, Lord,
> that once dry of all the dampness of this world
> the waters of life may fill us –
> O let your Spirit burn in our souls!

V – Love the Abjection

What a blessing is the emptiness of heart we find in our distaste for all things of this world, for this void the Lord fills with His presence. And what a blessing it is when creatures forsake us, for then the farewell to them is so much simpler. How we should love our abjection!

Help us, Lord, to traverse this desert,
loving the emptiness you so readily fill.

VI – "Not My Will"

It is difficult to accept and thank the Lord for the afflictions we undergo, but the more we manage to do so, the greater our spiritual progress will be. It is the abnegation of self we seek, and so the anguish we must submit to, as did Jesus on the Cross.

In silence and in peace
let us be obedient to your will, O Lord,
whatever it may cost us.

VII – The Crucifying Gift

When one progresses in the spiritual life, being gifted with the blessing of simple recollection, suffering will follow to purify our faith. We must thoroughly forget ourselves and allow God to act upon us, and the fruit of such crucifixion we will know.

Lord, as long as you would have us suffer,
let us suffer, with you.

VIII – Hope against Hope

When encompassed by darkness, subject to horrible temptation, what can we do but look to God, calmly, and in peace? And if this is not possible, if peace escapes our senses, we must trust that the Lord is still with us... and submit to the trials upon us. They will bring good fruit.

> O Lord, teach us always to fear you,
> yet never to be anxious about your justice
> or our own misery
> but always to wish to love and serve you
> and to desire death rather than to sin.

IX – Holy Abasement

What a heap of misery we are, what an abyss of corruption! And so we would remain if not for the mercy of God. In utter abasement let us stay as the Lord pulls up the noxious weeds of our self-love; let us realize our nothingness that He might fill the immense void in our souls with His divine life. If He seems to reject us as we suffer upon this cross, let us remember that the more hidden His love, the more profound it becomes.

> O Lord, in our agony come to us;
> leave us not alone.
> Sharing in your weakness
> we shall triumph.

X – Do Nothing

We must let God act upon us. We must join Jesus in His Passion. How blessed are those who know such great deprivation, who find the treasure that nothingness is. It is very painful to our corrupted nature, to our pride, to do nothing, and thus comes the blessing. For thus is our pride destroyed. By this death we come to eternal life in the Lord.

> O Lord, help us to let you tie our hands and feet
> and to remain at peace in such chains,

knowing you hide yourself from us
only to be more present to us.
Let this mortification bear its fruit.

XI – Keep in Repose

When seeking the Lord, we must be careful not to act on our own but allow Him to act upon our soul. Simply meditate on the life of Christ. Continually we must become aware of the truth of our own nothingness, but it should not disturb us – we should nourish pure charity and so love ourselves as we would our neighbor or even our enemy. In this is truth.

Lord, help us to allow all to pass through us
but pure love of you.

XII – God Remains Always

To teach us of His undying presence, to lead us to eternal life, the Lord allows us to undergo the cruelest of tortures, that any attachment to our lower nature might die and He might bring divine life to our souls. And so, though suffering terrible agonies, though on the rack expecting the end at any time... yet should we rejoice as the martyrs that all trust in ourselves is being crucified and we are finding absolute confidence in God, who lives forever.

O Lord, you never die
and we shall never die
as long as we sacrifice our lives for you.

XIII – Despairing of Love

God permits interior torments that our soul might be purified to its inmost recesses; and perhaps the greatest torment is when the Lord seems to take His mercy from us and love us no more. But in such annihilation we should rejoice, for in this darkness there is no fear of illusion and no opportunity for us to spoil His grace. Trust in the Lord – He never leaves us. Simply wait for Him.

> O Lord, make our will one with your own –
> teach us to love you even when
> your love seems gone from us.

XIV – The Second Death

We must all die to nature, to the senses and their pleasures – this is the ordinary course of holiness. But the Lord desires from chosen souls a death also to spiritual consolations, for He desires their love for Him to be unmixed with anything else: we must love Him alone.

Let us, as far as we can, leave behind any self-love, any self-seeking, and endure the annihilation we must know to join ourselves wholeheartedly to our all-good God.

> Repugnant as this second death may be,
> help us, O Lord, to suffer it all
> for that blessed peace
> that comes only by union with you.

XV – No Assurance

God makes us walk in darkness and humiliation with Him that we might recognize His absolute dominion; and though He leaves us without assurance about our salvation, once we submit to Him, we find great consolation: a firm hope founded in the infinite mercy of Christ and known by the light of faith. We come in this way to what is essential, to God Himself. And though there is still fear, it is peaceful; and though we still know our weakness, it but serves to keep us from the vanity of self-love.

> O Lord, help us to find you alone;
> as we are stripped of all attachments,
> let us see your Kingdom before our eyes.

XVI – Hidden Confidence

When our soul cries out for its lack of hope in the Lord's salvation, we should not confuse this with the despair of the damned who forsake God. In this cry from the depths of its darkness, the soul does not reject God but rather longs for Him more deeply than any other and exhibits great confidence in the presence of the Lord, which is hidden from it at that time.

> O Lord, may all understand the cry of the poor,
> the destitute who beg for you,
> and may you quickly answer our call.

XVII – Hidden Intention

If it is our desire to abandon ourselves to the Lord, He sees it and knows it, and this desire becomes a better act than any other, for it is deepest within us, where God dwells. And so, though we find no consolation, no apparent recognition of our abandonment, but rather find ourselves abandoned by Him... we should not fear – simply remain in humble recollection waiting on Him always.

> O Lord, more meritorious is that which rests upon pure faith,
> that which is hidden,
> for all things you see and know,
> and so you know best what is deepest within us.

XVIII – Perfect Confidence

We should give ourselves entirely to the Lord and rest in Him, knowing that He does always what is best for us and so we have cause for perfect trust. Distrust is for ourselves, and spiritual humiliation is the state for which we should strive before our God. Let us forget ourselves that we might find our true self in the Lord.

> O Lord, if we think of you,
> how much more will you think of us
> and provide all we need
> to bring us to union with you in Heaven.
> We place all our confidence in you.

OTHER BOOKS by JAMES KURT

"TURN and Become like Children":
Refuting the Presumed Contradictions of
the Jerusalem Bible Old Testament Commentary –
A case study recounting the problems afflicting modern biblical scholarship as found in the JB. 188 pp. 2019.

Prayers to the Saints (Updated) –
A page of prayer to each saint on the General Roman Calendar for the United States.
237 pp. 2019 (original 2007). w/ imprimatur.

Our Daily Bread:
Exposition of the Readings of Catholic Mass –
A page of writing for every Mass of the liturgical calendar for the Roman Rite; reflections drawn from the readings.
727 pp. 2004. w/ imprimatur.
Our Daily Bread: Lent – 86 pp. 2019. w/ imprimatur.

Remembrance of Things Present –
A mystical work seeking the presence of the LORD in the moment, where He dwells at all times.
100 pp. 2018. w/ imprimatur.

Two Books: Paradox and the Christian Faith/
Hippie Convert –
The apparent contradictions of the Faith are explained for those who seek wisdom; and a member of the flower generation addresses true love and peace, in poetic form.
238 pp. 2016. w/imprimatur.

Lines of Grace:
Meditations on Verses of Holy Scripture,
The Stations of the Cross, and The Most Holy Rosary –
A Catholic devotional especially for the encouragement of the practice of plenary indulgence. 195 pp. 2016.

Christian Vision of the Old Testament –
Synopsis and exhortation; faith-filled overview of all books of the Old Testament as prefiguration of Jesus, with a focus on the prophetic nature of God's Word.
273 pp.   2013.   w/ imprimatur.

Blessed Guilt: A Universal Conversion Story –
Extended parable on the life-giving repentance found in Jesus' blood; vaguely autobiographical but without particulars.   119 pp.   2013.   w/ imprimatur.

Chapters of the Gospels –
Exposition of the four gospels, chapter by chapter; in the style of *Our Daily Bread*.
114 pp.   2009.   w/ imprimatur.

*The Most Holy Trinity
and the Four Corners of the Universe* –
A collection of writings on the Trinity
and its reflection in Creation; founded upon the Shema.
300 pp.   2008.   w/ imprimatur.

YHWH: Order of the Divine NAME –
On the significance of the contemplative silence that is the NAME of God, and its application to a spiritual life.
260 pp.   2008.   w/ imprimatur.

Turn of the Jubilee Year: A Conversion Song –
Autobiographical depiction of vocation search through pilgrimage to Medjugorje and stays at a hermitage or two.
230 pp.   2004.

Songs for Children of Light: Ten Albums of Lyrics –
A white on black conceptual work with simple drawings for each song.   150 pp.   2003.

silence in the city –
Short contemplative poems; moments of divine silence in the midst of city life.   148 pp. (74 pieces).   2003.

www.ingramcontent.com/pod-product-compliance
Lightning Source LLC
Chambersburg PA
CBHW021638080526
44584CB00015BA/1540